7550

D1222266

APR   2010

21st Century Junior Library

WORKING AT THE AIRPORT

by Katie Marsico

CHERRY LAKE PUBLISHING * ANN ARBOR, MICHIGAN

CHERRY LAKE
Publishing

Published in the United States of America by Cherry Lake Publishing
Ann Arbor, Michigan
www.cherrylakepublishing.com

Content Adviser: Dr. Richard P. Hallion, Aerospace Historian
Reading Adviser: Cecilia Minden-Cupp, PhD, Literacy Consultant

Photo Credits: Page 4, ©iStockphoto.com/mikdam; page 6, ©iStock.com/impactimage; cover and page 8, ©Jeff Greenberg/Alamy; cover and page 10, ©Hugo de Wolf, used under license from Shutterstock, Inc.; page 12, ©iStockphoto.com/eejay62; cover and page 14, ©iStockphoto.com/VanWyckExpress; page 16, ©iStockphoto.com/Nikontiger; page 18, ©Serghei Starus, used under license from Shutterstock, Inc.; cover and page 20, ©iStock.com/bbossom

LIBRARY OF CONGRESS CATALOGING-IN-PUBLICATION DATA
Marsico, Katie, 1980–
  Working at the airport / by Katie Marsico.
     p. cm.—(21st century junior library)
  Includes index.
  ISBN-13: 978-1-60279-510-5
  ISBN-10: 1-60279-510-X
  1. Airports—Juvenile literature. 2. Airports—Employees—Juvenile
literature. I. Title. II. Series.
  HE9797.M37 2010
  387.7'36—dc22   2008049547

*Cherry Lake Publishing would like to acknowledge the work of
The Partnership for 21st Century Skills.
Please visit www.21stcenturyskills.org for more information.*

CONTENTS

Have you ever been to an airport? What did you
see when you looked out the window?

What Is an Airport?

You pull your bags to the window and look outside. You can see huge airplanes all over the **runway**. One of them moves closer to your window. You will get on this plane in a few minutes. Where are you? You are at the airport!

Some workers make sure that all the parts of the plane are working.

People go to airports when they travel by plane. Some people fly across the country. Others travel all over the world.

Who do you ask if you have questions at the airport? Airport workers can help answer your questions!

Create!

Draw a picture of your local airport. Be sure to include drawings of all the workers you see there. You may discover that more people work at the airport than you thought!

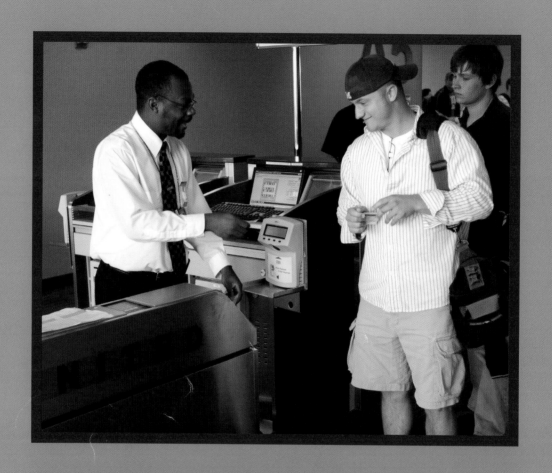

Workers at the gate make sure people are getting on the right plane.

Airport Workers

Who do you talk to when you get to the airport? You speak to a **ticket agent**. He looks at your ticket. He also helps you with your luggage. The ticket agent can tell you which gate you need to find. You will board the plane at the gate.

Security workers look closely at suitcases. They want to make sure there is nothing unsafe in them.

You will meet **security workers** on your way to the gate. They make sure you follow some simple rules that will keep everyone safe. Security workers look carefully at anything you bring on the plane. They work very hard to make sure that you are safe. They are happy to answer any questions you might have.

Some controllers work in special airport towers.

Controllers are important airport workers. They give instructions to pilots. They help them land their planes safely.

Controllers also give directions to workers on the runway. The runway is a busy place. Planes are moving back and forth. People often drive trucks and cars between these planes. Controllers make sure that everyone on the runway has enough space to do their jobs safely.

Baggage handlers need to be strong. They have to move heavy suitcases.

Does anyone else work at the airport? Yes! Many different workers are at an airport. **Baggage handlers** load and unload luggage on planes. **Mechanics** fix any planes that have broken parts. They also check to make sure that planes are safe. **Custodians** help keep the airport clean. They pick up trash. They also vacuum the airport and clean the restrooms.

It takes a lot of hard work and training to become a pilot.

On the plane, you might see the **pilots** and **flight attendants**. The pilot and copilot fly the plane. Flight attendants make sure passengers have a safe and enjoyable flight.

Make a Guess!

Guess how many people work at your local airport. Write down your guess. The next time you visit the airport, ask a worker if he knows the answer. Was your guess correct?

Many flight attendants speak more than
one language.

Do You Want to Work at the Airport?

Does working at an airport interest you? This is something you can start thinking about now. Talk to some workers the next time you visit the airport. Also, find out if an airport near you offers tours.

Ask Questions!

Ask questions when you are at the airport. Talk to the ticket agent about why she chose her job. Ask the flight attendant what he likes best about his work. This will help you learn more about jobs that interest you.

Some workers make sure planes have enough fuel.
People do many different jobs at the airport.

Watch the airport workers doing their jobs. You may learn that many airport workers enjoy traveling. Most are good at helping other people. An airport can be an exciting place to work. Learn as much as you can now. Then you can decide if working at the airport is right for you!

GLOSSARY

baggage handlers (BAG-ij HAND-lurz) workers who load and unload luggage on planes

controllers (kun-TROLL-urz) workers who make sure that airplanes move safely in and out of airports

custodians (kuhsss-TOH-dee-uhnz) workers who clean the airport

flight attendants (FLITE uh-TEN-duhntz) workers who look after travelers once they get on the plane and during their flight

mechanics (muh-KAN-iks) workers who fix airplanes

pilots (PYE-luhtz) workers who fly planes

runway (RUHN-way) a strip of ground where planes take off and land

security workers (si-KYOOR-ih-tee WUR-kurz) workers who check luggage and speak to travelers to make sure that no one and nothing will hurt anyone on the plane

ticket agent (TIH-ket AY-juhnt) a worker who helps travelers with their plane tickets and luggage

FIND OUT MORE

BOOKS

Hutchings, Amy. *What Happens at an Airport?* Pleasantville, NY: Weekly Reader, 2009.

Minden, Cecilia, and Mary Minden-Zins. *Pilots*. Chanhassen, MN: The Child's World, 2006.

WEB SITES

Philadelphia International Airport—Kid's Corner
www.phl.org/kids_corner.html
Learn about how planes fly, discover the aviation alphabet, and find cool games and puzzles

U.S. Department of Labor and U.S. Department of Education—Career Voyages: Transportation—Air
www.careervoyages.gov/transportation-air.cfm
Read about different jobs at the airport, including what skills you will need to work there

INDEX

ABOUT THE AUTHOR

Katie Marsico is the author of more than 50 children's books and lives in Elmhurst, Illinois, with her husband and children. She would especially like to thank workers at the Chicago Airport System for helping her research this title.